AF791121

Instant jQuery Drag-and-Drop Grids How-to

A practical, hands-on guide to building drag-and-drop layouts using Gridster, jQuery, and CSS

Marcos Placona

[PACKT] PUBLISHING

BIRMINGHAM - MUMBAI

Instant jQuery Drag-and-Drop Grids How-to

First published: March 2013

Production Reference: 1200313

Published by Packt Publishing Ltd.
Livery Place
35 Livery Street
Birmingham B3 2PB, UK.

ISBN 978-1-78216-500-2

`www.packtpub.com`

Credits

Author
Marcos Placona

Reviewers
Caleb Evans
Yousuf Qureshi
Gabriele Romanato

Acquisition Editor
Erol Staveley

Commissioning Editor
Maria D'souza

Technical Editor
Soumya Kanti

Copy Editor
Alfida Paiva

Project Coordinator
Joel Goveya

Proofreader
Maria Gould

Graphics
Aditi Gajjar

Production Coordinator
Melwyn D'sa

Cover Work
Melwyn D'sa

Cover Image
Aditi Gajjar

About the Author

Marcos Placona grew up in São Paulo, Brazil, and started tinkering with web development when 14.400 kbps modems were the coolest thing. He then engaged on a Computer Science degree, but a better opportunity arose on the other side of the Atlantic. In his 20s, he then decided to move to England where he worked as a ColdFusion developer and started blogging at `www.placona.co.uk`.

After acquiring a taste for mobile application development, he has now published over 20 applications on all the major mobile markets, and hopes he will someday see a kid on the train playing one of his games.

He is now working as a technical lead for HolstelBookers where he tries to stay on top of its ColdFusion and .NET teams, as well as designing solutions and working with the stakeholders to turn dreams into reality.

> My efforts in this book are dedicated to my family. Special thanks to my lovely wife Cilene who was understanding and supportive while I tried to juggle my day-to-day work, my studies, and this book at the same time. Also thanks to my friends at Packt Publishing.

About the Reviewers

Caleb Evans is a freelance web developer from Carlsbad, California. He currently attends college in pursuit of a Computer Science degree, and in his free time, he maintains a personal website and a collection of web applications. He has a growing knowledge of a number of web technologies, including HTML5, CSS3, JavaScript, and PHP, with which he builds many of these web apps.

Caleb is also the lead developer of jCanvas, a powerful jQuery plugin designed to extend the capabilities of the HTML5 canvas. Thcsc capabilities include animation, drag-and-drop, vectors, and a slew of customizable parameters. You can check it out at `calebevans.me/projects/jcanvas/`.

Yousuf Qureshi graduated with a BSc (Hons) in Computing and Software Engineering from Leeds Metropolitan University, Leeds UK. He is an early adopter of technology and gadgets, and has deep experience in the e-commerce, social media, social networking, and mobile apps sector.

His expertise includes development, technology turnaround, consultancy, architecture, and development of Android, iOS, Blackberry, ASP.NET MVC, JAVA, jQuery, Node.js, Oracle ADF, Windows 8 apps, Media API integration, and multiplatform applications.

Currently he focuses on the big data platform, NoSQL databases, and Hadoop.

In particular, I'd like to acknowledge my parents, who encouraged my work and got it moving.

Gabriele Romanato is a web developer with over eight years of experience. Particularly skilled with JavaScript, CSS, jQuery, PHP, WordPress, and many web standards, he currently works as a freelance developer in sunny Italy. He blogs at `http://blog.gabrieleromanato.com/` on the not so subtle art of web development.

I'd like to thank my family for all their support during these years. I'd also like to thank Stefano Campioli, Paolo Loschi, Francesco "Franz" Zoboli, and Simone Nava at Wamboo for being the best friends a simple developer could have.

Table of Contents

Preface

Gridster is a drag-and-drop jQuery plugin that allows users to build interactive layouts from elements spanning multiple columns. Its API permits users to easily implement draggable elements on their layouts for highly customizable pages.

As users, we all have certain preferences when it comes to browsing the Internet. I will describe three typical website users in the following list that can be found browsing any website.

- **Content-sensitive users**: These are the ones for whom all that matters when visiting a website is the content it presents. They don't care too much about presentation, and are usually only after the information it has to give. We geeks will rapidly fall into this category, but news websites will also attract this type of user. Think how often you stopped reading the news to think about the website's layout.
- **Highly visual users**: These users will mostly keep visiting a website if it is visually attractive, and will rapidly lose interest when presented with too much information and no "eye-candy". Under this category, you will usually find users without much "web ability"; that is, your grandma and your uncle Bob.
- **Browsing users**: Our third and final category for this example is the browser. While it may seem like I'm talking about web browsers here, what I am really trying to describe are the shoppers. These kind of users are normally relentless, and don't care about what's in front of them as long as they can buy it. Don't talk to them about how much your pet shop likes animals, but give them something to buy (and obviously deliver it), and they will be your friends forever.

Now, the bottom line here is that we are trying to satisfy three very different kinds of users, and as of now, there's just no way the good old "header -> left-nav -> content" layout will make any of them happy.

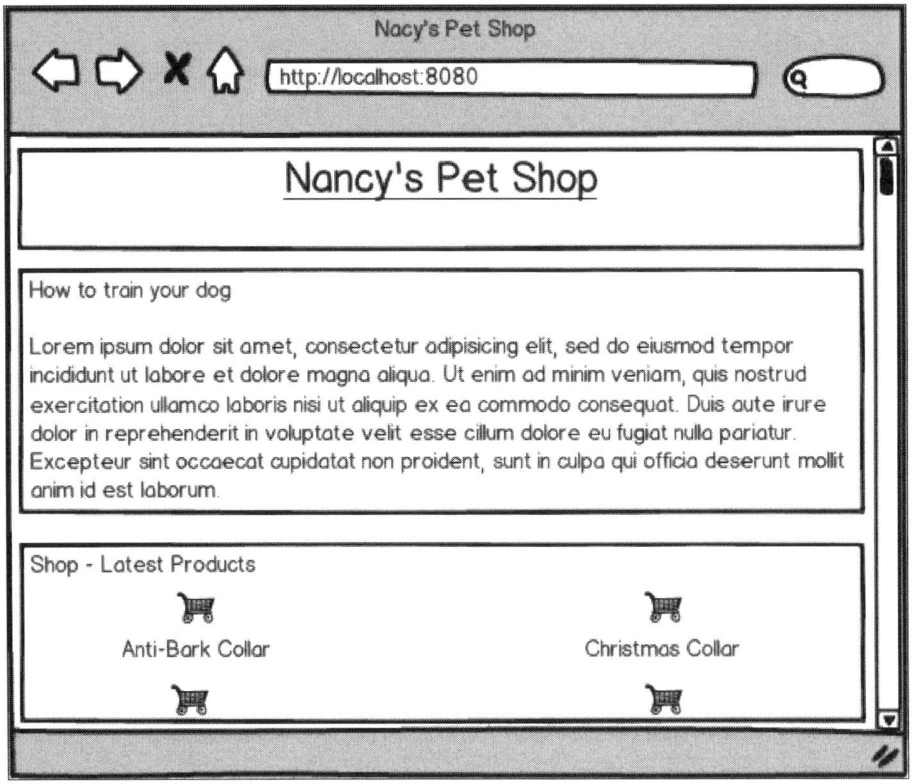

The image represents the typical static interface a user could be presented with prior to implementing Gridster.

What if I told you that with Gridster you can do all that and much more? After reading this book, you will be able to cater to the three user stereotypes previously described, and many others you can think of. So let's jump headfirst in to what you need to do to get Gridster up and running in no time.

What this book covers

Preparing your website to use Gridster describes all the necessary steps to get Gridster running on a simple webpage.

Your first Gridster layout shows you how to build your first simple Gridster-draggable layout.

Understanding initialization options describes all the important initialization options required to give Gridster the desired look and feel.

Using Gridster callbacks describes how to use event-driven functionality to track the user's behavior.

Using Gridster methods describes how to use API methods to make layouts more dynamic and enables you to control your widgets at runtime.

Building a draggable layout using Gridster shows you how to build a fully-featured, draggable layout using metro-style.

What you need for this book

The only tool you will need for this book is any text processing software such as Notepad, Textpad, Visual Studio, and so on. You will also need to have basic knowledge of HTML, CSS, and JavaScript. Having had some exposure to jQuery is desirable but not mandatory since the book will take you through the basics.

Who this book is for

This book is aimed at developers and designers willing to create highly dynamic websites where user interaction is key. The book only covers client-side code; therefore, it isn't necessary to have previously worked with any server-side technologies.

Conventions

In this book, you will find a number of styles of text that distinguish between different kinds of information. Here are some examples of these styles, and an explanation of their meaning.

Code words in text are shown as follows: "We can include other contexts through the use of the `include` directive."

A block of code is set as follows:

```
$(document).ready(function(){ //DOM Ready
  var gridster = $(".gridster ul").gridster({
    widget_margins: [10, 10],
    widget_base_dimensions: [100, 100]
  });
});
```

New terms and **important words** are shown in bold. Words that you see on the screen, in menus or dialog boxes for example, appear in the text like this: "clicking the **Next** button moves you to the next screen".

[Warnings or important notes appear in a box like this.]

[Tips and tricks appear like this.]

Reader feedback

Feedback from our readers is always welcome. Let us know what you think about this book—what you liked or may have disliked. Reader feedback is important for us to develop titles that you really get the most out of.

To send us general feedback, simply send an e-mail to `feedback@packtpub.com`, and mention the book title via the subject of your message.

If there is a topic that you have expertise in and you are interested in either writing or contributing to a book, see our author guide on `www.packtpub.com/authors`.

Customer support

Now that you are the proud owner of a Packt book, we have a number of things to help you to get the most from your purchase.

Downloading the example code

You can download the example code files for all Packt books you have purchased from your account at `http://www.packtpub.com`. If you purchased this book elsewhere, you can visit `http://www.packtpub.com/support` and register to have the files e-mailed directly to you.

Errata

Although we have taken every care to ensure the accuracy of our content, mistakes do happen. If you find a mistake in one of our books—maybe a mistake in the text or the code—we would be grateful if you would report this to us. By doing so, you can save other readers from frustration and help us improve subsequent versions of this book. If you find any errata, please report them by visiting `http://www.packtpub.com/submit-errata`, selecting your book, clicking on the **errata submission form** link, and entering the details of your errata. Once your errata are verified, your submission will be accepted and the errata will be uploaded on our website, or added to any list of existing errata, under the Errata section of that title. Any existing errata can be viewed by selecting your title from `http://www.packtpub.com/support`.

Piracy

Piracy of copyright material on the Internet is an ongoing problem across all media. At Packt, we take the protection of our copyright and licenses very seriously. If you come across any illegal copies of our works, in any form, on the Internet, please provide us with the location address or website name immediately so that we can pursue a remedy.

Please contact us at `copyright@packtpub.com` with a link to the suspected pirated material.

We appreciate your help in protecting our authors, and our ability to bring you valuable content.

Questions

You can contact us at `questions@packtpub.com` if you are having a problem with any aspect of the book, and we will do our best to address it.

Instant jQuery Drag-and-Drop Grids How-to

Welcome to *Instant jQuery Drag-and-Drop Grids How-to*. By using this book, you will be able to learn all the ins and outs of drag-and-drop, multi-column layouts, as well as being able to develop a fully functional metro-style layout that allows you to drag-and-drop all of its elements and reposition them however you would like.

Preparing your website to use Gridster (Simple)

This recipe will describe all the necessary steps to get Gridster up and running on your website, as well as demonstrate how to include any of the dependencies needed by the library.

Getting ready

There are only two things needed to get Gridster installed on your source code. You first need to download jQuery if you don't already have it, and then download the latest version of Gridster. After that, you will use plain HTML code to include both libraries in your webpage.

For most casual users, adding the latest version of jQuery will suffice. There are also nightly builds available, but these won't be discussed here as they are not necessary, and the latest version should be able to do everything we need.

How to do it...

1. Start by visiting jQuery's website, `http://jquery.com/download/`, and download the library to a location you will remember. We won't be debugging our jQuery code in the examples given in this book, so downloading the production version will be fine.

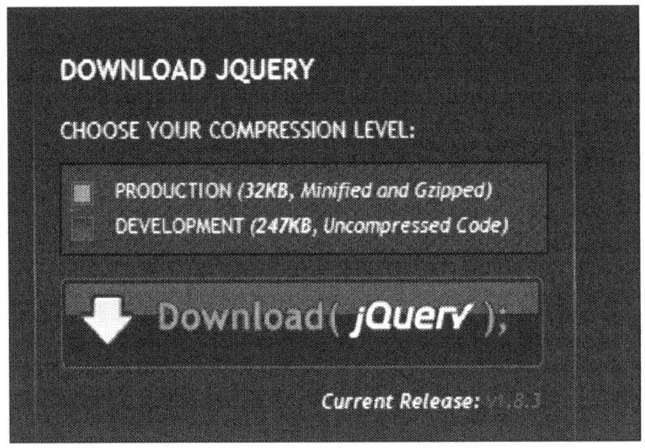

2. We should now head over to Gridster's website, `http://gridster.net/#download`, and download the minified versions of both the `gridster.js` and `gridster.css` files. These are the files we will use throughout this entire book, so make sure they are kept safe and accessible. A suggestion would be to create a directory structure to make it easier to refer to the files. I will be using the following structure for the examples given here:

3. Under the directory **recipe1**, create a new text file called `index.html`. This file should initially contain the following code:

```
<!DOCTYPE html>
<html>
```

```
<head>
<script src="../scripts/jquery-1.8.3.min.js"></script>
<script src="../scripts/jquery.gridster.min.js"></script>
<link href="../styles/jquery.gridster.min.css" rel="stylesheet" />
<title>Recipe 1</title>
</head>
<body>
  Hello Gridster!
</body>
</html>
```

[You can download the example code files for all Packt books that you have purchased from your account at `http://www.packtpub.com`. If you purchased this book elsewhere, you can visit `http://www.packtpub.com/support` and register to have the files e-mailed directly to you.]

4. By double-clicking on this file, you should be presented with a screen that looks like the following screenshot:

5. You can check that everything has loaded up correctly by pressing the *F12* key on your browser (Chrome or Firefox), and checking that all files have been correctly loaded without errors, as shown in the following screenshot:

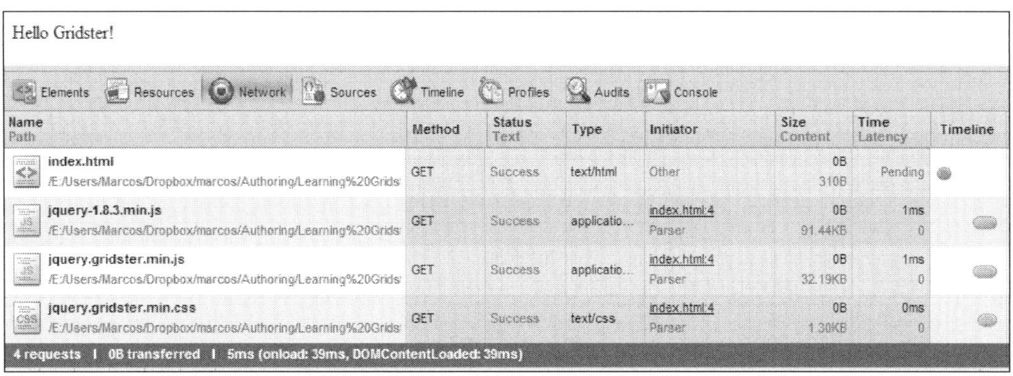

There's more...

Instead of downloading the files into your project, you can simply load them up via CDN-hosted copies of the files, as follows:

```
<script src="https://ajax.googleapis.com/ajax/libs/jquery/1.8.3/
jquery.min.js">
</script>
```

In that case, the files wouldn't be coming from your website, but from jQuery's website itself. This is a good practice when trying to improve performance, as big web servers tend to host files on multiple locations and use very aggressive caching techniques to make sure the files are served quickly.

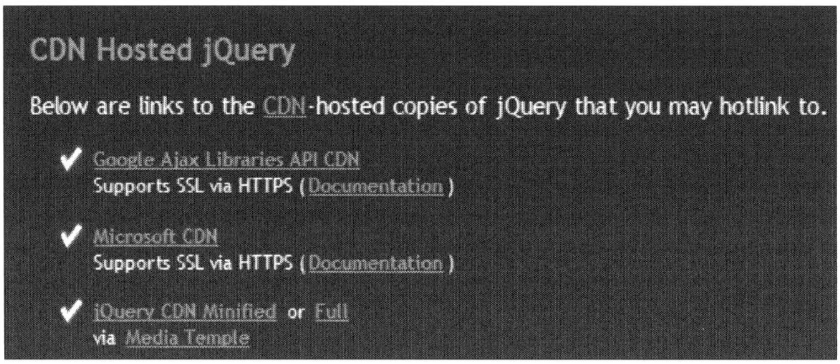

Gridster also offers files in the same way from their website as you will find in their download section. So, for example, you could link directly to their minified file as follows:

```
<script
src="https://raw.github.com/ducksboard/gridster.js/master/dist/
jquery.gridster.min.js">
</script>
```

Your first Gridster layout (Intermediate)

In this recipe we will now build a simple draggable layout. The idea of this recipe is to give you a taste of how draggable layouts work, and how much you can accomplish with very little code.

At the end of this tutorial, we should end up with a draggable layout that looks as follows:

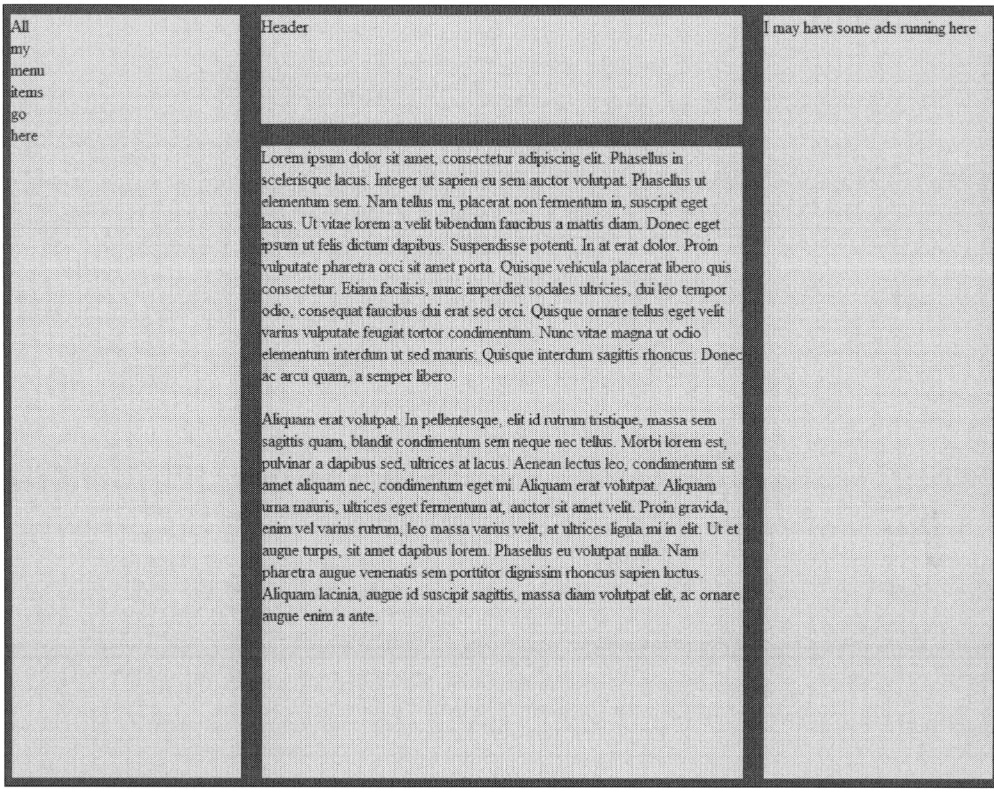

Getting ready

We have already downloaded all the necessary libraries to complete this recipe as part of the recipe, *Preparing you website to use Gridster (Simple)*. To make things easier, we can now simply copy the contents of the **recipe1** directory into the **recipe2** directory, and do a bit of cleaning up as follows:

```
<!DOCTYPE html>
<html>
<head>
<script src="../scripts/jquery-1.8.3.min.js"></script>
<script src="../scripts/jquery.gridster.min.js"></script>
<link href="../styles/jquery.gridster.min.css" rel="stylesheet"
type="text/css" />
<title>Recipe 2</title>
</head>
<body>
```

```
</body>
</html>
```

As you can see, we only modified the title of the recipe, and removed the contents of the body as we won't need it. It is important that all the library imports are still kept intact, as your code will not run without them.

How to do it...

This is where the fun begins. We will now start by adding the HTML items to our `index.html` file.

1. We will start by creating a `div` element on our page to hold our grids together. This step is very important, as all the CSS code will be loaded into the Document Object Model (DOM) based on this `div` tag. It is also important that the `class` attribute is called `"gridster"`, as this will allow for the library to refer to the correct element.
2. Within this `div` tag, we will also create a `ul` element, and four list items inside this `ul` element. You should end up with code inside your `body` tag that looks like this:

```
<div class="gridster">
  <ul>
    <li></li>
    <li></li>
    <li></li>
    <li></li>
  </ul>
</div>
```

The HTML output isn't very impressive, but the magic is just about to start happening, and we will be dragging these items in no time.

If you have the following list items showing up on your browser, congratulations! You have done very well so far, and from here on things will get a lot cooler.

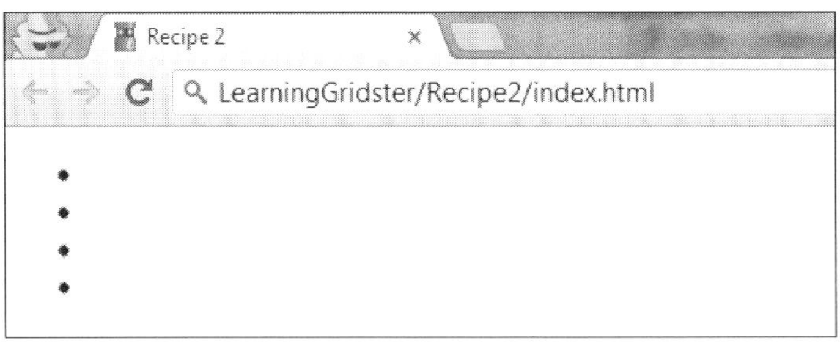

Each one of those bullets are actual bits of our layout. Believe it or not!

3. Now let's go ahead and modify our list's items in order to tell Gridster what each one of them represents. We will add four attributes to each of our list items:
    - `data-row`: This represents the row where we want the item to be displayed; so in a five-row layout, if the `data-row` attribute of the first element was specified as `3`, the first and second rows would have been empty, and the element would be shown on position three.
    - `data-col`: This is the counterpart of the `data-row` attribute, but specifies in which column an element will be displayed. Similar to the previous example, if an element had its `data-col` attribute specified, this would dictate its position within the layout.
    - `data-sizex`: This attribute defines the width of a given element. The number you use here is a multiplier to the defined values you use during the initialization of your layout.
    - `data-sizey`: This attribute defines the height of a given element. Just like the `data-sizex` attribute, this is merely a multiplier to the number used during your layout's initialization. We will cover initialization in more depth from now on.

4. Now it's time to modify our list items to define the necessary attributes as shown in the following code snippet:

```
<div class="gridster">
  <ul>
    <li data-row="1" data-col="1" data-sizex="2"
data-sizey="6"></li>
    <li data-row="1" data-col="1" data-sizex="4"
data-sizey="1"></li>
    <li data-row="1" data-col="1" data-sizex="4"
data-sizey="5"></li>
    <li data-row="4" data-col="6" data-sizex="2"
data-sizey="6"></li>
  </ul>
</div>
```

The following image represents each of the rows and columns in which we placed our elements:

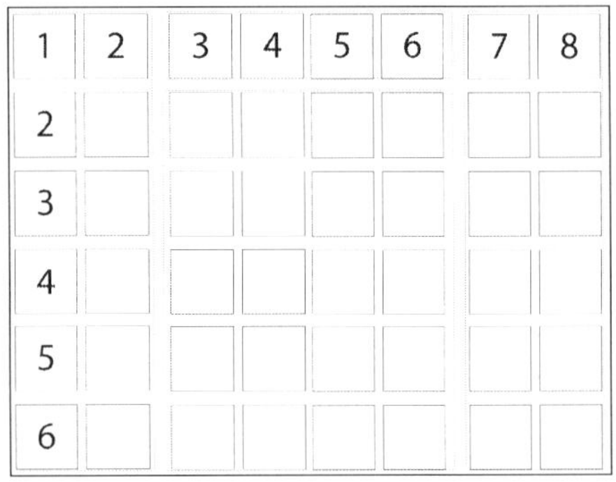

As you can see from the previous image, all the pieces come together naturally, but if you want to have them separated by gaps, it would then be very important that you set all the positions first. The following example shows you a different grid with spaces between each of the items:

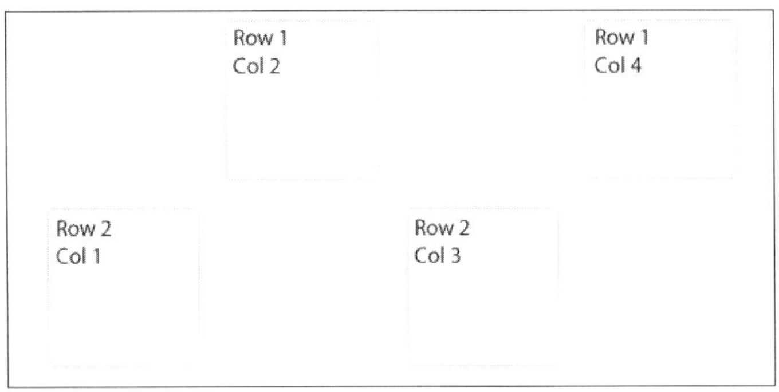

5. The code for inserting spaces within the item would then look like the following:

```
<div class="gridster">
  <ul>
    <li data-row="2" data-col="1" data-sizex="1"
data-sizey="1"></li>
    <li data-row="1" data-col="2" data-sizex="1"
data-sizey="1"></li>
    <li data-row="2" data-col="3" data-sizex="1"
data-sizey="1"></li>
    <li data-row="1" data-col="4" data-sizex="1"
data-sizey="1"></li>
  </ul>
</div>
```

If you have executed any of the code we have written together so far, you will have noticed that not much is actually happening on the screen. This is because we are yet to initialize our layout via the **Gridster API**. So let's not waste any more time and get coding.

```
$(document).ready(function(){ //DOM Ready
  var gridster = $(".gridster ul").gridster({
    widget_margins: [10, 10],
    widget_base_dimensions: [100, 100]
  });
});
```

6. If you refresh your page on the browser at this point, you should be presented with the following image:

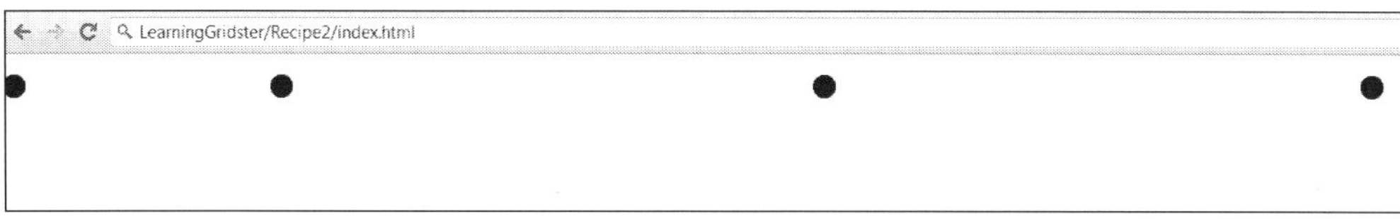

Believe it or not, this is your layout, but it still doesn't have any styling. If you try clicking on any of the dots on the screen and dragging them around, you should see that they actually move.

7. All we need to do now is add some style to it, which we will do with CSS using the following CSS code:

```
<style>
/*
  Our list items should not have the regular dots
*/
ul {
    list-style: none;
}
/*
  Set out layout to be 960px wide
*/
.gridster {
    width: 960px;
    margin: 0 auto;
}
/*
  Give the layout a boxy look with shadows, and
  change the cursor over the elements so it's
  easier to know where to drag
```

```
*/
.gridster .gs_w {
    background: #FFF;
    cursor: pointer;
    box-shadow: 0 0 5px rgba(0,0,0,0.3);
}
</style>
```

If you followed this recipe up to here, you should now have something like this on your screen:

How it works...

It's important to notice here that we purely described each and every attribute for completeness. If we didn't want to declare the row and column position here, we could have completely omitted it, since all the objects end up being aligned naturally as they all come exactly after each other. We have started our layout by simply adding plain HTML elements into the DOM.

We then moved on by decorating these elements with attributes, which dictate where to position them on the screen.

Once all our elements were correctly positioned, we initialized Gridster, and "told" it exactly where to find the elements we wanted it to turn into draggable objects. We did this by making the following declaration:

```
$(".gridster ul")
```

We also had to tell Gridster how much spacing we wanted between each of the elements, and did so by using the `widget_margins` initialization option.

In the previous example, we set it to be `[10, 10]`, which means 10 pixels from the top, and 10 pixels from the left on each element.

The last thing we had to do in the initialization was to declare how high and wide we wanted each of our rows and columns to be by using `widget_base_dimensions`.

We have used 100 x 100 pixels for the height and width, as it would make it easier for us to make sure everything was nicely displayed on the screen.

Lastly, we added some CSS code to our page so that we're able to visualize each of our objects as an actual layout item.

All Gridster elements have the `gs_w` class added to them, so we can manipulate them with CSS. We've used it in our favor to add some shadows and change the cursor on our elements.

There's more...

All of the list items are simply styled as HTML elements, which means you can do whatever you want with them. So, for example, you could start adding content into them, such as menu items, images, plain text, or even more HTML objects.

The following CSS code would make the element's colors alternate between black and yellow:

```
.gridster .gs_w:nth-child(odd) {
  background: #000;
}
.gridster .gs_w:nth-child(even) {
  background: #FF0;
}
```

This would make our position-alternating example from the beginning of this recipe look like this:

Understanding initialization options (Intermediate)

We have already used two initialization options in the previous recipe when declaring the element spacing and dimensions by using the `widget_margins` and `widget_base_dimensions` options. We will now explore the most important options we can use to make our layouts even better.

> All initialization parameters are optional, but using them will improve the look and feel of your layout.

Getting ready

We will start by looking at what some attributes do, and then apply them to basic examples.

Let's copy all the contents from the **recipe1** directory, and clear the code up like we did in **recipe2**. I could have simply provided you with a template here, but we want to familiarize ourselves with all the aspects of building draggable layouts.

Our code should look like the following after some cleanup:

```
<!DOCTYPE html>
<html>
<head>
<script src="../scripts/jquery-1.8.3.min.js"></script>
<script src="../scripts/jquery.gridster.min.js"></script>
<link href="../styles/jquery.gridster.min.css" rel="stylesheet"
type="text/css" />
<title>Recipe 3</title>
</head>
<body>
</body>
</html>
```

We will soon talk about adding some action to our layout, but let's first go a step back and understand what each option gives us:

- `widget_selector`: This option defines the draggable widgets on the page. While in the previous example we have used unordered lists, you could use any HTML element; however, I find lists easier to work with.
- `widget_margins`: These are the margins you will want to have between your widgets. It gets defaulted to 10px (left, right) by 10px (top, bottom). It receives an array, such as `[10,10]`, as its value.

- `widget_base_dimensions`: This property specifies the base size of your widgets and works as a template size for all your widgets. So, for example, if you wanted to have a widget that was 300 px wide, and had specified that the `widget_base_dimensions` attribute is `[100, 100]` (100 px wide by 100 px high), you could simply specify the `data-sizex` attribute of your widget to `3`, and this would be equal to 300 px.
- `max_size_x`: This option specifies the maximum size a widget can have. If specified `5`, any widget with a `data-sizex` attribute value above that will be ignored.
- `serialize_params`: This option tells Gridster to keep track of the position of each object on the screen, and allows you to retrieve this information for later usage. This is very useful when saving user layout preferences.

We can now create a few simple widgets on the screen that will illustrate the usage of the initialization options previously described.

How to do it...

1. We will start by adding some JavaScript code to our code with the initialization arguments.

> Remember, initialization options act like a contract. Your HTML can only contain options and values that are allowed by them.

```
$(function(){ //DOM Ready
  var gridster = $(".gridster ul").gridster({
    widget_margins: [5, 5],
    widget_base_dimensions: [100, 100],
    max_size_x:1,
    serialize_params: function($w, wgd) {
      return {
        col: wgd.col,
        row: wgd.row
      };
    }
  }).data('gridster');
});
```

2. We will now go ahead and modify our HTML to have the following list items:

```
<div class="gridster">
  <ul>
    <li data-row="2" data-col="1" data-sizex="1"
data-sizey="1"></li>
    <li data-row="1" data-col="2" data-sizex="1"
```

```
data-sizey="1"></li>
    <li data-row="2" data-col="3" data-sizex="1"
data-sizey="1"></li>
    <li data-row="1" data-col="4" data-sizex="1"
data-sizey="1"></li>
  </ul>
</div>
```

3. Now go ahead and copy the CSS you've created for the recipe, *Your first Gridster layout (Intermediate)*. We won't need to do any modifications to it other than adding some colors as suggested at the end of the *Your first Gridster layout (Intermediate)* recipe. This is to make it a bit more visual:

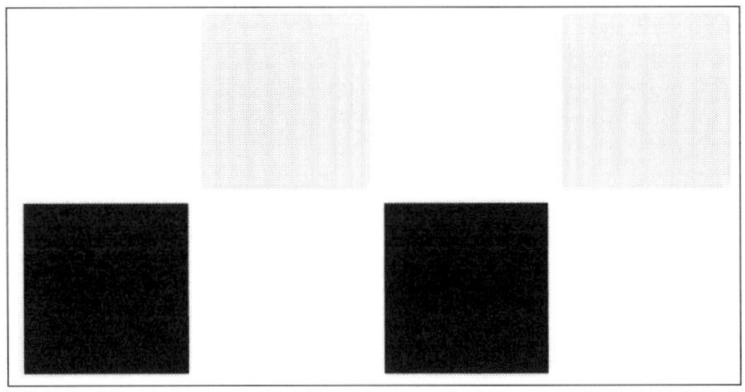

How it works...

As you have seen from the previous example, we have used all the same initialization options that we described earlier. We define the margins (`widget_margins`) for each of our widgets to be `[5,5]`, then the width and height (`widget_base_dimensions`) to be `[100,100]`.

Next, we defined the maximum width (`max_size_x`) for each of our widgets. This is to guarantee that any widgets that are defined above that size are ignored by our layout. This is especially useful if you let your users create custom widgets and don't want the layout to go outside of the boundaries with massive widgets.

> You could also have used the property `max_size_y` to limit the height of the widgets.

Lastly, we used the `serialize_params` option to enable our layout to report on each of its elements. This is particularly useful when saving user preferences as we will see in the next few recipes. We used the code to report the column and rows on which each of our widgets are.

There's more...

If you can't wait to see exactly what the `serialize_params` option does, you can add some debugging lines to your code, and you will be able to see exactly the location of our widgets.

All you need to do is create a new HTML element on your code of type `button`:

```
<button class="check" id="check">check</button>
```

We now need to add some action to this button, as by itself it will just be sitting on the page without doing much.

So add the following code to your JavaScript block:

```
$('#check').bind('click',function() {
  console.log(gridster.serialize());
  return false;
});
```

The previous code simply binds the `'click'` function to your button, and it uses JavaScript's logging capabilities to display the contents of a given object.

If you now run your code in the browser and press the *F12* key to display the debugging panel and select **Console**, you should be able to click on the **check** button and see that a new entry is added to the console as follows:

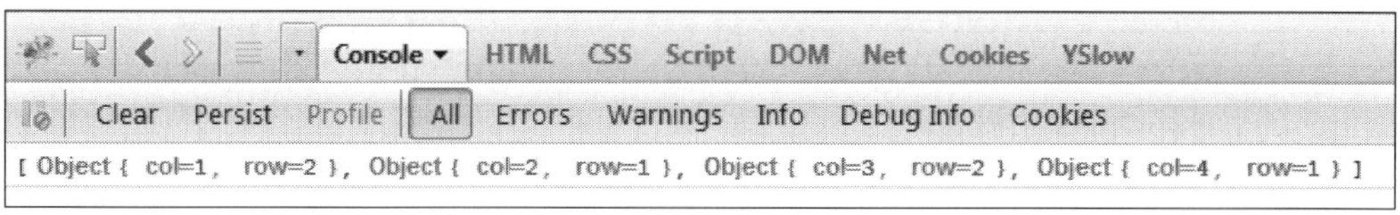

If you then move any of the widgets on the screen, and press the **check** button again, you should now see that the values on the console have been updated to match what you have on the screen at present.

Using Gridster callbacks (Advanced)

Gridster comes bundled with some JavaScript callbacks that can be integrated within every layout. In this recipe, we will go through a few of them, and show through simple examples what can be accomplished with their usage.

Callbacks are events that get triggered when the user interacts with the page. When those events are initiated, there are certain functions that enable us to identify them and act upon them.

Getting ready

We will start by looking at some of the available functions, and then write a simple application that uses all of them together with the help of the debugger. The callbacks we will be looking at are for dragging (draggable) detection, and are as follows:

- `start`: This function gets executed every time a widget is dragged. It will only be executed once until the mouse is released.
- `stop`: This function is the opposite of the previous function, and gets triggered whenever a widget was just stopped from being dragged.

> Combine the previous two functions, and you will know exactly when a widget was started or was stopped from being dragged.

- `drag`: This function is triggered whenever a widget is being dragged. It will be called multiple times until the mouse is actually released, and the widget is no longer being dragged. If you defined the `stop` function in your initialization, this function will then be called.

How to do it...

1. We will now start coding this recipe by copying the contents from the *Understanding initialization options (Intermediate)* recipe. We won't be changing anything in the HTML and CSS code, but we will only be adding more initialization options to the JavaScript.
2. Right after where we have the `serialize_params` option, add a comma and type the following code:

```
draggable: {
  start: function(event, ui){
    // your start events here
    console.log('started');
  },
  stop: function(event, ui){
    // your stop events here
    console.log('stopped');
  },
  drag: function(event, ui){
    // your dragging events here
    console.log('dragging');
  }
}
```

3. If you now run this code on the browser, you should see that the same example that we saw in the previous recipe has loaded.

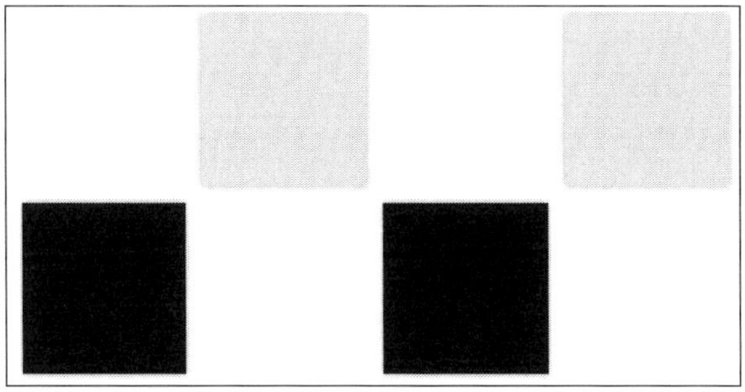

4. When dragging any of the items, you should be able to check the browser console (by pressing the *F12* key) and verify that all the events are being tracked and passed as output on the log:

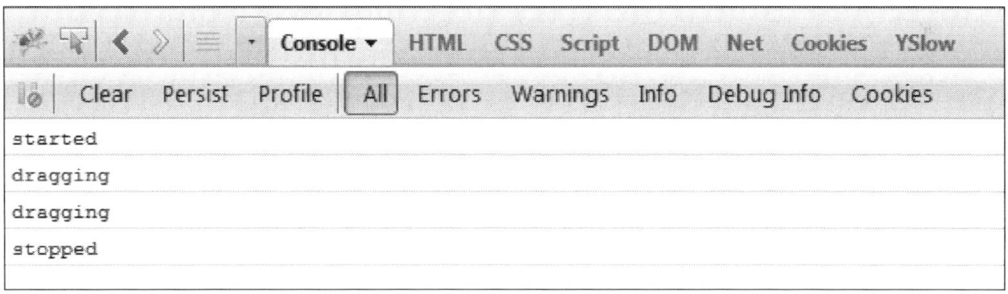

How it works...

As you will have seen, every time you drag one of the items, there will be some debugging information being logged. We are currently capturing this by adding a message to the log describing which event was triggered, but you could have added anything in there.

Gridster has some very clever event listening capabilities. By adding the methods previously described to the initialization of your layout, you are basically telling it to keep an eye on anything that happens to the layout, and whenever it detects any modifications to it, it will report back to any of the pre-defined functions (`start`, `stop`, and `drag` in our case), and if they have any actions assigned to them, those will happen.

Each of the functions receive two arguments. We called them `event` and `ui`, but those can be called anything you want.

The `Event` attribute holds information about what action is being taken against our layout. In this case, the action is "touch", as shown in the following screenshot of the code, since we are grabbing an item and trying to move it from one place to another. This is especially good for building mobile applications, as they will automatically work when users touch their screen and try to drag an item.

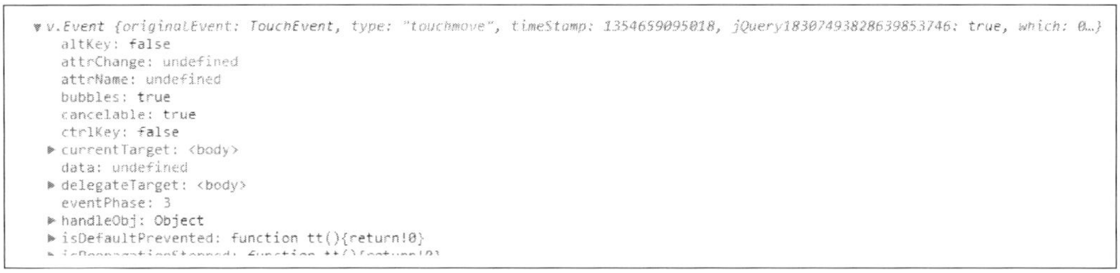

The `ui` argument, on the other hand, has information about the item itself being dragged. By inspecting the `ui` element, you will see that the x and y coordinates as well as the dimensions and object type are registered on it, as shown in the following screenshot of the code:

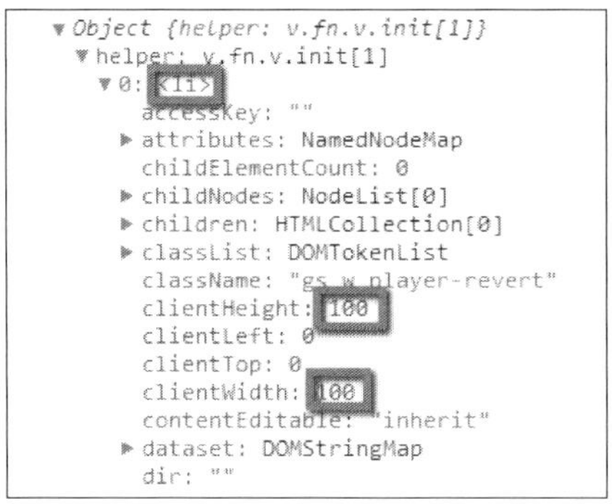

There's more...

Gridster also offers a collision API, which is likewise draggable, thereby allowing you to identify when certain items have collided with other items. So, for example, you could trigger a callback whenever a certain item of your layout had collided with another one, giving the user a message that this type of action isn't supported and is likely to cause undesired effects to your website.

Like the draggable methods, you can detect whenever an item starts colliding with another, stops colliding, or is currently colliding.

Using Gridster methods (Advanced)

There are a few methods available in Gridster's API. These methods enable developers to be create or modify grid layouts at runtime. In this recipe, we will go through some of the important methods and exemplify their usage along with the parameters they receive.

Until now, we have only worked with predefined layouts, which means every widget within our layout has been created by us prior to the page being loaded. We will now change this, and allow the users to go on and create widgets at runtime.

Getting ready

We will start by copying the contents of the *Using Gridster callbacks (Advanced)* recipe. All the files should remain the same, and we will only make a few changes to them in order to create dynamic widgets on our layout. Make sure you run the HTML file in it and check that everything still works. In this recipe we will assume that you have a draggable layout that looks like the following image:

We will now remove the initialization option `max_size_x` from the JavaScript so that we don't have any limitations as to the size in which we want to create our dynamic widgets, and also the complete draggable block, since we don't need to track dragging events in this recipe.

We are going to use the following six methods in this recipe:

- `add_widget`: This method creates a new widget on a given grid. You can specify a string of an HTML element that you would like to create (that is, `<li>test</li>`), the dimensions such as width and height, and which column and row you would like it to be created in, as shown in the following code:

  ```
  .add_widget( html, [size_x], [size_y], [col], [row] )
  ```

- `resize_widget`: This method allows you to resize an existing widget by specifying the HTML element, the width, and height, as shown in the following code:

  ```
  .resize_widget( $widget, [size_x], [size_y] )
  ```

> In the previous code, `$widget` is a reference to the object you would like to resize; it could be something like `$('.header')` if your widget had the class `"header"` assigned to it.

- `remove_widget`: This method does the exact opposite of adding a dynamic widget to the grid, as it will remove a widget from the grid when given an element's reference. You can also use a callback to let the user know when a certain widget has been removed from the grid, as shown in the following code:

  ```
  .remove_widget( $widget, callback )
  ```

  The callback could be any function you'd like, such as the one shown in the following code:

  ```
  function(){console.log('removed item')}
  ```

- `serialize`: This method inspects our widgets in order to get their column and row value, just like we saw back in the *Understanding initialization options (Intermediate)* recipe. We did that by using a combination of `serialize_params` methods to tell Gridster to keep track of our widgets, and then calling `.serialize` at the end to output those values on the debugger.

  ```
  .serialize( [$widgets] )
  ```

  It will, by default, serialize every widget on your grid, but you can specify single widgets that you wanted to serialize.

- `disable`: This method allows you to disable the dragging of any of the objects inside your grid using the following code:

  ```
  .disable( )
  ```

  Objects will not be draggable until you re-enable them.

- `enable`: This method does the opposite of the previous method. While grids will start enabled by default, you could change your logic to restart all grids which were disabled, and then only allow certain people to interact with them by calling this method using the following code:

  ```
  .enable( )
  ```

  > Notice that all method arguments within square brackets are non-mandatory.

  If your grid has been disabled, all items will become draggable once you call `enable`.

How to do it...

Let's now modify our JavaScript to put all the new methods we learned about into practice.

1. We will start by adding five new buttons to our HTML page. They will go with the existing `"check"` button. We will define them in the following way:
   - `<button class="add" id="add">add</button>`
   - `<button class="resize" id="resize">resize</button>`
   - `<button class="remove" id="remove">remove</button>`
   - `<button class="check" id="check">check</button>`
   - `<button class="disable" id="disable">disable</button>`
   - `<button class="enable" id="enable">enable</button>`
2. If you run your HTML page on the browser, you should now have six buttons under your grid. The only one that actually does something is the `"check"` button, as we have already implemented its functionality back in the *Understanding initialization options (Intermediate)* recipe.
3. Just like we did previously for the `"check"` button, we need to bind a `'click'` event to each of our buttons. We will use the following code for now:

```
$('#add').bind('click',function() {
  // our action goes here
  return false;
});
```

4. We should repeat the previous code four more times, one for each of the remaining `"resize"`, `"remove"`, `"disable"`, and `"enable"` buttons.
5. After implementing bind events for each of the buttons you have created, you should now end up with code that looks like this:

```
$(function(){ //DOM Ready
  var gridster = $(".gridster ul").gridster({
    widget_margins: [5, 5],
    widget_base_dimensions: [100, 100],
    serialize_params: function($w, wgd) {
    return {
      col: wgd.col,
      row: wgd.row
    };
  }
}).data('gridster');

// add
```

```
$('#add').bind('click',function() {
  /*
  creating a new list-item element and adding 'new_widget' as
  its class. We also define this widget will have a "sizex" and
  "sizey" of 1
  Lastly we define the column and row we would like our widget
  to be positioned
  */
  gridster.add_widget("<li class='new_widget'></li>", 1, 1, 5, 2);
  return false;
});

// resize
$('#resize').bind('click',function() {
  /*
  We use a selector to indicate wich widget we would like to
  resize. We then say this widget will have a "sizex" and a
  "sizey" of 2.
  */
  gridster.resize_widget($('.new_widget'), 2, 2);
  return false;
});

// remove
$('#remove').bind('click',function() {
  /*
  We use a selector to indicate which widget we would like to
  remove.
  */
  gridster.remove_widget($('.new_widget'));
});

// check
$('#check').bind('click',function() {
  console.log(gridster.serialize());
  return false;
  });

// disable
$('#disable').bind('click',function() {
  gridster.disable();
});

// enable
```

```
    $('#enable').bind('click',function() {
      gridster.enable();
      });
    });
```

How it works...

If you run this code on your browser, you will notice that whenever you click on the "add" button, a new item is created on the rightmost corner of your grid. You can then manipulate this item by using the resize functionality to make it bigger, or you can remove it altogether, but you've not got the ability to enable and disable your entire grid with the click of a button.

Each one of the described methods integrates seamlessly with Gridster's API. Whenever you create a new HTML element in your code, Gridster is behind the scenes calling the very same methods that you have just used; it's just that you can't see it.

We are now benefiting from that by calling those methods whenever we want, and allowing the user to decide where and when a new element will be created in the layout.

With this in mind, you could also skip the entirety of writing the HTML code, and add all your elements via JavaScript by calling the method `add_widget`.

This is especially useful when saving the user's preferences; you will want to let the user choose where to position each of the elements, and then create them at runtime the next time they loaded the page, by creating all the items dynamically.

You could also use initialization options to make sure that dynamically created items get created according to what you specified during the initialization.

There's more...

As we have seen previously, Gridster methods are really powerful and allow you to do the same with JavaScript as you could do with HTML. The following example shows how to create our four-square layout, but only with the aid of JavaScript, to add the elements to the grid.

Our HTML would only need to have the parent `ul` item to hold our elements, as shown in the following code:

```
<div class="gridster">
  <ul></ul>
</div>
```

Our JavaScript would have the same initialization options, but all the widgets should be added dynamically via API calls using the following code:

```
$(function(){ //DOM Ready
  var gridster = $(".gridster ul").gridster({
    widget_margins: [5, 5],
    widget_base_dimensions: [100, 100]
  }).data('gridster');

  // create all the items in runtime
  gridster.add_widget("<li></li>", 1, 1, 1, 2);
  gridster.add_widget("<li></li>", 1, 1, 2, 1);
  gridster.add_widget("<li></li>", 1, 1, 3, 2);
  gridster.add_widget("<li></li>", 1, 1, 4, 1);

})
```

Building a draggable layout using Gridster (Intermediate)

This recipe aims to explain and exemplify how a draggable layout can be built. After completing this recipe, you should end up with a fully usable metro-styled layout.

Getting ready

We will start this recipe by making a copy of the contents of the last recipe, and removing some things we won't need.

You can start by removing the logic added to our CSS code to alternate colors between black and yellow. We will be setting our own colors here.

Now, also clear out all the contents from the script element as we will be writing a much more simplified initialization here, and will define this layout mostly via HTML code.

How to do it...

1. Let's start by adding some predefined colors to our stylesheet. We will use these colors in each of our tiles so that they look like truly metro-styled tiles.

   ```
   // purple
   .gridster li.purple{
     background: #A200FF;
   }
   ```

2. As we will be adding some icons to our widgets, let's work on some of its alignment:

```
.gridster img{
  display: block;
  margin-top:20px;
  margin-left: auto;
  margin-right: auto
}
```

3. We will now create one of the previous code blocks for each of the colors. You should end up with ten blocks, one for each of the following colors: purple, magenta, teal, lime, brown, pink, orange, blue, red, and green.

Color Name	**Hexadecimal code**
Purple	#A200FF
Magenta	#FF0097
Teal	#00ABA9
Lime	#8CBF26
Brown	#A05000
Pink	#E671B8
Orange	#F09609
Blue	#1BA1E2
Red	#E51400
Green	#339933

That should be it for the CSS coding part of this recipe.

4. We will now move on to the HTML code and define a `div` tag and an unordered list as we have done previously with the other recipes using the following code. I will assume you have already imported all the necessary assets as you've done before.

```
<div class="gridster" id="gridster">
  <ul></ul>
</div>
```

5. Within this unordered list, we will create our widgets. In this case, I will opt to create the widgets via HTML coding as opposed to define them via JavaScript. This is because we will want to add images and extra styles to our widgets, and while we could do this via JavaScript, doing it via HTML is just a little bit more readable and easy to understand.

```
<ul>
  <li data-row="1" data-col="1" data-sizex="2" data-sizey="1"
class="blue"></li>
  <li data-row="2" data-col="1" data-sizex="2" data-sizey="1"
```

```
class="magenta"></li>
  <li data-row="3" data-col="1" data-sizex="2" data-sizey="1"
class="purple"></li>
  <li data-row="4" data-col="1" data-sizex="2" data-sizey="1"
class="teal"></li>
  <li data-row="1" data-col="3" data-sizex="2" data-sizey="1"
class="lime"></li>
  <li data-row="2" data-col="3" data-sizex="2" data-sizey="1"
class="brown"></li>
  <li data-row="3" data-col="3" data-sizex="2" data-sizey="1"
class="pink"></li>
  <li data-row="4" data-col="3" data-sizex="2" data-sizey="1"
class="orange"></li>
  <li data-row="1" data-col="5" data-sizex="1" data-sizey="1"
class="red"></li>
  <li data-row="2" data-col="5" data-sizex="1" data-sizey="1"
class="green">
  </li>
  <li data-row="3" data-col="5" data-sizex="2" data-sizey="1"
class="blue"></li>
  <li data-row="4" data-col="5" data-sizex="1" data-sizey="1"
class="magenta"></li>
  <li data-row="1" data-col="6" data-sizex="1" data-sizey="1"
class="purple"></li>
  <li data-row="2" data-col="6" data-sizex="1" data-sizey="1"
class="pink"></li>
  <li data-row="4" data-col="6" data-sizex="1" data-sizey="1"
class="brown"></li>
</ul>
```

6. The final part will be to create the JavaScript code; we won't need to do anything special here, as we have defined all of our widgets via HTML in the previous step. The following block of code should suffice:

```
$(function(){ //DOM Ready
  var gridster = $(".gridster ul").gridster({
    widget_margins: [5, 5],
    widget_base_dimensions: [100, 100]
  });
});
```

7. If you run your code in the browser, you should now have a layout that looks like this:

And obviously, every item on the grid is draggable, so try it out.

How it works...

We have defined the initial position of all of our items; using those positions the items were aligned correctly, and made sure about positioning them in order.

In the previous example, we need to remember that the widget positioned to the right of the leftmost one is in reality at position three (even though it's the second to be shown). That is because our first widget occupies two positions (as defined by the command `data-sizex="2"`).

We add all the colors manually to each of our widgets. This is to guarantee that the colors are spread out evenly.

All the classes for each of our ten colors have been defined by using the following code:

```
.gridster li.mycolor{
  background:#some_hex;
}
```

We try to be as unintrusive as we can, so we're saying that every list item (`li`) within the Gridster div tag that uses the class (`mycolor` in the previous example) will have a background as defined by our hex code.

We are also preparing each of our widgets to have an image inside of them. We use a little CSS trick to align it 20 px from the top, and center it.

The easiest part of it is to add some JavaScript code to initialize our grid. Like we've done before, we're simply defining a 5 px gap between each of the widgets, and telling Gridster every widget is 100 px wide by 100 px high.

There's more...

You will probably be asking yourself why we have defined margins for images placed inside our widgets. Having them allows us to have a very nice looking grid, as shown in the following screenshot:

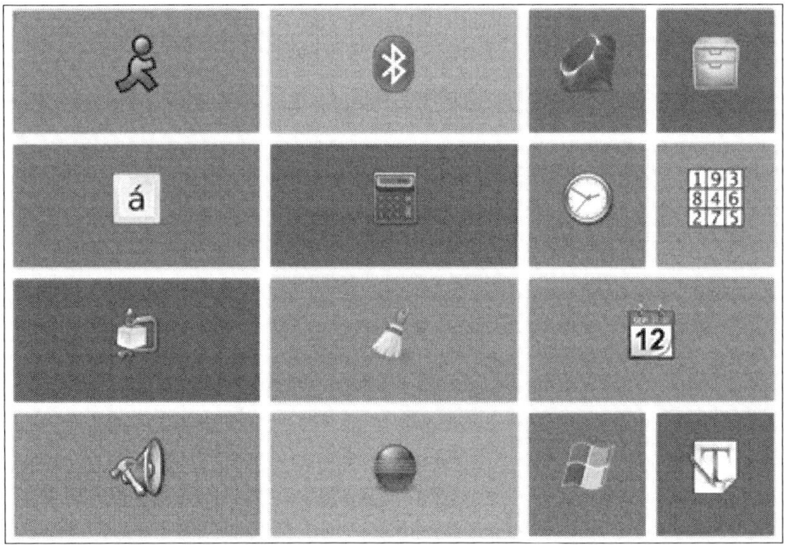

All I did in this case was add some `img` tags inside of each of the list items, and defined which image I wanted to have displayed.

[PACKT] PUBLISHING

Thank you for buying Instant jQuery Drag-and-Drop Grids How-to

About Packt Publishing

Packt, pronounced 'packed', published its first book "*Mastering phpMyAdmin for Effective MySQL Management*" in April 2004 and subsequently continued to specialize in publishing highly focused books on specific technologies and solutions.

Our books and publications share the experiences of your fellow IT professionals in adapting and customizing today's systems, applications, and frameworks. Our solution based books give you the knowledge and power to customize the software and technologies you're using to get the job done. Packt books are more specific and less general than the IT books you have seen in the past. Our unique business model allows us to bring you more focused information, giving you more of what you need to know, and less of what you don't.

Packt is a modern, yet unique publishing company, which focuses on producing quality, cutting-edge books for communities of developers, administrators, and newbies alike. For more information, please visit our website: `www.packtpub.com`.

Writing for Packt

We welcome all inquiries from people who are interested in authoring. Book proposals should be sent to `author@packtpub.com`. If your book idea is still at an early stage and you would like to discuss it first before writing a formal book proposal, contact us; one of our commissioning editors will get in touch with you.

We're not just looking for published authors; if you have strong technical skills but no writing experience, our experienced editors can help you develop a writing career, or simply get some additional reward for your expertise.

[PACKT] PUBLISHING

jQuery for Designers: Beginners Guide

ISBN: 978-1-849516-70-9 Paperback: 332 pages

An approachable introduction to web design in jQuery for non-programmers

1. Enhance the user experience of your site by adding useful jQuery features
2. Learn the basics of adding impressive jQuery effects and animations even if you've never written a line of JavaScript
3. Easy step-by-step approach shows you everything you need to know to get started improving your website with jQuery

---

jQuery UI Themes Beginner's Guide

ISBN: 978-1-849510-44-8 Paperback: 268 pages

Create new themes for your jQuery site with this step-by-step guide

1. Learn the details of the jQuery UI theme framework by example
2. No prior knowledge of jQuery UI or theming frameworks is necessary
3. The CSS structure is explained in an easy-to-understand and approachable way

Please check **www.PacktPub.com** for information on our titles

2387469R00026

Made in the USA
San Bernardino, CA
15 April 2013